I0202160

INSIDE THE SWAN TOMB

Oliver Bestul

Ten|16
PRESS
www.ten16press.com - Waukesha, WI

INSIDE THE SWAN TOMB
Copyrighted © 2019, 2022 Oliver Bestul
ISBN 978-1-64538-019-1
Second Edition

INSIDE THE SWAN TOMB
by Oliver Bestul

All Rights Reserved. Written permission must be secured from
the publisher to use or reproduce any part of this book, except for
brief quotations in critical reviews or articles.

For information, please contact:

Ten|16
PRESS

www.ten16press.com
Waukesha, WI

Cover art by Ginny Prince

This book is a work of fiction. Names, characters, places and
incidents are the product of the author's imagination or are used
fictitiously. Characters in this book have no relation to anyone
bearing the same name and are not based on anyone known or
unknown to the author. Any resemblance to actual businesses
or companies, events, locales, or persons, living or dead, is
coincidental.

Original Cast

Oliver Best...Oliver Bestul

Killian Coffin.................................Killian Coffinet

Veronica Swan..........................Veronica Swanson

INSIDE THE SWAN TOMB

[London, 1832. All is dark. A small flame enters from offstage]

KILLIAN   Hello? Hello?

OLIVER   Hello yourself, Son, and mind that wedge. It keeps the tomb door open. [A pause] What is it?

KILLIAN   I thought for a moment there was someone in here with us.

OLIVER   There is. [The stage is alighted, revealing a coffin on a marble base and two men. The younger, Killian, in black, the older, Oliver, in grey, an old twisted scar running the length of his head and neck, holding a candle. They are in a small room with a single door, propped ajar with a wedge] This is a home we've come to raid. [Pouring a drop of wax from the end of his candle, Oliver affixes it to a corner of the marble base. He then removes a bag from his shoulder and sets it down]

KILLIAN   Whose? [A long door on the side of the coffin opens slowly to the audience, unnoticed by the men. Inside lies Veronica, apparently dead, wearing a black ribbon around her neck, dressed in a white wedding dress]

OLIVER   [Pointing to the coffin] Hers – so soon are the dead forgotten!

KILLIAN   Yes, the *dead*. Veronica's body alone inhabits that coffin, just as dead as one of the nails in it. [He pounds once on the coffin lid. Veronica awakes with a gasp, breathing heavily and feeling around blindly] Homes are built for those who live.

VERONICA   [Unheard by the men and in a strained voice] Hello?

OLIVER   *Veronica*, daughter of the sexton Swan, that Owl of Saint Augustine. *Veronica Swan*, then?

KILLIAN   Yes.

OLIVER   That's the second name I've known. [He produces a crowbar and hammer from his bag, and begins intermittently to hammer and pry at the lid of the coffin, working his way around it]

VERONICA   Hello? [The audience-facing door slams shut, silencing Veronica's breathing]

KILLIAN   How could that be so? What's the first, your own?

OLIVER   No, no. The names of the exhumed, I mean. The bodies. She's the second one I've known the name.

KILLIAN   The first?

OLIVER   [A pause] My first robbery.

KILLIAN   Who was he?

OLIVER   She. She was a – a lover of mine, taken sick. The Owl assisted me.

KILLIAN   *You* worked with Master Swan? [Pointing to the coffin] Her father?

OLIVER   The same. The first of many in twenty years of two-man robberies. [Killian ponders this] He told me – [Catching himself]

KILLIAN   What did he say?

OLIVER   He told me if I saw her that way, my lover, in the grave, I could always think of her as only sleeping.

KILLIAN   [Coldly] You bastard.

OLIVER   That's my business.

KILLIAN   You absolute *scoundrel*! When you said to me those very words and brought me in *here*, I thought it an act of charity! Fool that I was! You wanted only to find yourself another partner, yes? Now that Master Swan has ceased this life of petty thievery?

OLIVER   [Sardonically] Oh yes, oh pity petty me! Bless the noble Owl for buying instead this cemetery, affording his life of *virtuous* luxury! Ha! Had he not, he'd still be with me robbing, the fiend!

KILLIAN   Hold your tongue or I'll have it! What was I thinking, entering a tomb with a lunatic? I'm *leaving*. [He turns to do so]

OLIVER   I know what you were thinking. [Killian pauses] You thought, 'Perhaps the world, or God, has only played a trick on me. She's not dead, not my lover, not mine. She's waiting there inside.' [A pause] You can call me a scoundrel, but when I watched from the shadows as the Owl's carriage left tonight, and when I scaled the cemetery wall alone for what I knew would be my final robbery, only to find you sitting outside the tomb weeping, I knew somehow you belonged in here with me.

KILLIAN   Your final robbery?

OLIVER   I too am leaving, Son, leaving London. I left my soul in Halifax, see, and I intend to retrieve it. But the Owl, he owes me this body. [Pointing to the coffin] He owes me twenty years of them, but this one, his family, especially.

KILLIAN   [A pause] I'll stay.

OLIVER   [Setting the hammer and crowbar down, now across the tomb from his bag] So help me. Take that end. [They remove the coffin's lid]

KILLIAN   [Surprised for a moment] The lead
second coffin, I'd forgotten it.

OLIVER   There should be a saw and a pick
in that bag. [Killian produces the implements
and hands them to Oliver] And what of *your*
first, Son? [He gestures toward the coffin] Who
was she to you? [He stabs a hole into the lead
with his pick, above Veronica's head. A pause]
What, a lover also, was it?

KILLIAN   A lover, yes, also taken sick. [Oliver
fits the tip of his saw into the hole in the lead,
then begins cutting an opening, three sides of
a square, into it] It's a funny feeling, speaking
forevers as children then, and now . . . and
seeing her dead. [To himself] She loved me,
I'm sure, through her sickness.

OLIVER   Yes – yes I'm sure she did.

KILLIAN   [A pause] What about the stones?

OLIVER   Which? [Having finished cutting, he takes up his crowbar again, prying up the edge of the rough hatch door he has cut from the lead]

KILLIAN   Those over the bodies you've stolen, the gravestones. How is hers the second name you've known?

OLIVER   [He begins with his hands to fold the hatch door further open] I can't read. [A hand reaches out from inside the coffin and grabs his wrist. Oliver falls to the ground] Good God!

KILLIAN   [Cautiously peering over the half-open hatch door, he startles and wrenches it shut again] What is this!

OLIVER   [To himself] Amy?

KILLIAN   A *trick*! A trick indeed! Not of God or the world, of you and she! [He points to Oliver and the coffin in succession]

OLIVER   [Again to himself] Was that my Amy? [The hatch door of lead is pushed up again, from the inside. Oliver rises to swing it open completely]

VERONICA   [Sticking her head up from the opening, and in the same strained voice] What's . . . What's happening? [Over the slow course of several lines, her voice returns to normality]

OLIVER   I *knew* you hadn't gone, I *knew* I was mistaken. There had been some sort of switch! I knew it, Amy! I always looked for you on our corner, I did. [Noticing her look of confusion] Amy . . .

VERONICA   Veronica. Veronica Swan, sir, sorry.

OLIVER   [To himself] What? A triplet?

VERONICA   [Noticing Killian] Killian, you look as if dressed for a funeral.

OLIVER   Yours.

KILLIAN   [To him] Speak not another word.

OLIVER   [To her] You're dead, girl.

KILLIAN   Quiet, I said!

VERONICA   Who is this man, Killian?

OLIVER   A resurrectionist, miss. Oliver Best.

KILLIAN   Resurrectionist, ha! As if the
position held a modicum of honor. *Best*, was
it? That's laughable, body-snatcher. You are the
worst man I have ever met.

VERONICA   It's true, then? Killian, am I dead?

KILLIAN   Veronica . . .

VERONICA   This room of stone, my tomb? This
box of lead, my coffin, Killian?

OLIVER   And I, and this *Killian,* here to remove you from it.

KILLIAN   Heed not a single word he says!

VERONICA   For what purpose, resurrectionist? To sell my body, is that it?

OLIVER   It is.

VERONICA   To the academy? To the anatomy students?

OLIVER   Yes, yes, for their dissections, miss. I meant no dirtiness, no disrespect.

KILLIAN   And yet you deal with pig anatomists.

OLIVER   'Know first thyself, presume not God to scan; The proper study of mankind is man.'

VERONICA   That's Pope, is it not?

OLIVER   The pope wrote that? You'd think he'd think God often scans.

KILLIAN   Alexander Pope, she means.

VERONICA   Father always *is* reciting it. 'The enemy, children, is not the anatomist, but the robber of graves. Anatomy is a noble profession. Know first thyself, presume not God to scan.'

OLIVER   Yes, I too have heard enough of it from him.

VERONICA   From Father, you mean? [A pause] Killian, who is this man?

KILLIAN   A demon.

OLIVER   Perhaps - as partner to the Owl of Saint Augustine.

VERONICA   My father works no longer as their sexton.

OLIVER   Yes, he purchased land for London's first cemetery and left his partner, me, abandoned. 'I'm sorry, Son,' he said, as if it would repay me. I know this story.

VERONICA   But you're mistaken. My father protected the buried from resurrections. He despised them, never joined them. You yourself call him the Owl.

OLIVER   And you understand how he received that name?

KILLIAN   For his benevolence, his wisdom as a sexton.

VERONICA   Yes!

KILLIAN   [To further convince Veronica] Because while every other churchyard overflows with corpses, that of Saint Augustine has been impeccably managed, by both myself *and* the Owl, as you call him.

OLIVER   So your connection's deeper than the romance I detected. I can tell you, Son, that there hasn't been a body buried at Saint Augustine for more than a few hours in almost two decades. Easy to find space when every coffin's unburied. I myself helped the Owl remove them.

VERONICA   Killian?

OLIVER   And he's called the Owl, because he was always in the churchyard at night –

KILLIAN   [Interrupting] Quite   right, Veronica. And he was always in the churchyard at night because he was guarding the graves.

OLIVER   [Interjecting] Robbing! Robbing the graves! And he's called the Owl, too, because of the bones he left of his victim.

KILLIAN   Silence, you!

VERONICA   What does he mean?

OLIVER   There was another resurrectionist, miss, who died by your father's hand, shortly after he and I went into business.

KILLIAN   Veronica, don't listen to this lunatic.

VERONICA   What happened to the man?

KILLIAN   What?

VERONICA   Resurrectionist, what happened to the man?

OLIVER   He found the Owl and myself at Saint Augustine one midnight, digging up the grave he'd also come to empty. All he said was 'Swan?' before your father had his hands around his neck. Choked to death. We sold two bodies that evening, and your father requested the bones of the resurrectionist back. He left them in a heap at the churchyard gate, below a sign that read *Discovered Body-Snatcher*. 'That's no sexton,' the people whispered, 'there's an owl at Saint Augustine.'

KILLIAN   The – the authorities never would have allowed it.

OLIVER   The London lawmen decided the sexton had done them a service. One less churchyard to patrol, miss.

VERONICA   Killian, did you know of this? My father, a resurrectionist?

OLIVER   He certainly didn't seem surprised to hear it, this Killian, when I mentioned it.

KILLIAN   Quiet! Quiet I said! Come, Veronica, I'll help you down and we'll leave him. [Reaching for her]

VERONICA   Don't touch me. I can rise myself, thanks. [She starts to rise from her coffin and notices what she's wearing] Is this my wedding dress? [A pause] Killian? Killian, why was I buried in it?

OLIVER   To who are you married, miss?

VERONICA   [Distracted, nodding in Killian's direction] To him. Engaged, I mean. My betrothed. Resurrectionist, what is the date?

OLIVER   End of April, miss. April twenty . . . twenty-seventh.

VERONICA   [A pause] Killian, what's happened? Were we wed today?

KILLIAN   There was an accident.

VERONICA   What accident? [She rises and steps uneasily from the coffin]

OLIVER   Mind that wedge. It keeps the tomb
      door open.

VERONICA   What accident, Killian?

OLIVER   [A pause] There's a ribbon, miss,
      about your neck, that doesn't match your dress.
      [He reaches for it]

KILLIAN   Don't! [Oliver pauses. Instead,
      Veronica unties the black ribbon and lets it
      fall, a fresh noose scar revealed. She feels it and
      winces in pain at the touch]

VERONICA   What happened?

OLIVER   [A pause] Hanged, miss.

VERONICA   Executed? Killian?

OLIVER   No, miss.

VERONICA   I didn't . . . I didn't . . . Not on purpose . . .

OLIVER   I've never known a soul to knot a noose on accident.

VERONICA   Killian?

KILLIAN   [Walking toward her] Veronica, we can go home. We can forget about it.

VERONICA   No – no! There's nothing to forget! I didn't do it! I know, Killian, I *know* I didn't do it! In my *heart*, Killian, I know it!

KILLIAN   Veronica, there was . . . there was no one else there when I found you in the basement.

VERONICA   Killian, you listen to me — you listen! Someone strung me up and blamed me for it! I swear it, Killian, I swear I would never do it!

KILLIAN   Did they do that too, [He points] to
          your head? [She feels her head, the short hair
          upon it]

VERONICA   Oh, oh Killian, who cut it? I'm sorry,
          you always loved it . . . Who cut it, Killian?

KILLIAN   [Angrily] You did! You did! [Sadly]
          You did.

VERONICA   [A pause] What did you do, Killian?
          To deserve this on your wedding day?

KILLIAN   I . . . I didn't do anything.

VERONICA   Why are you here tonight, Killian?
          [A pause] Killian?

KILLIAN   I wanted to – to see you again, to be
          with you.

VERONICA   [A pause] Forever, like you used to
          say?

KILLIAN   [A bit embarrassed] Of course, yes.
   [Veronica removes the wedge, and the tomb
   door slams]

VERONICA   Well that seals it, doesn't it, Killian?

KILLIAN   [Stunned] That door, it locks on its
   own.

VERONICA   I know.

KILLIAN   It locks on its own.

OLIVER   [Stunned] I need to go to Halifax.

VERONICA   I know.

OLIVER   About Halifax?

VERONICA   About the door . . .

KILLIAN   It locks on its own.

VERONICA   . . . not Halifax.

KILLIAN   It locks on its own.

VERONICA   What's there?

OLIVER   In Halifax?

KILLIAN   It locks on its own.

OLIVER   My soul.

KILLIAN   It locks on its own.

VERONICA   Killian, Killian.

KILLIAN   Yes?

VERONICA   I know.

OLIVER   Is there no other exit?

KILLIAN   [He gestures toward her] What

would she do with another exit? She's dead. *We're* dead, us three.

OLIVER   How thick are these walls?

KILLIAN   Two feet. Two feet thick.

OLIVER   Do you jest?

KILLIAN   The tomb was built as a model, for potential clients of Kingstead.

VERONICA   Kingstead! Father buried me at *Kingstead Cemetery*!

KILLIAN   Yours was the first interment on the premises. We've not yet opened to the public.

VERONICA   [Sarcastically] What a privilege it is.

OLIVER   And the door?

VERONICA   What?

OLIVER   Will it not open?

VERONICA   There is no keyhole, no handle on it.

KILLIAN   Not on our side. [A pause] It locks –

OLIVER   On its own, yes. Can we not break it?

KILLIAN   Three iron sheets, three inches thick,
              with gaps of air in between them. 'Unrobbable,'
              we've been telling all parties interested. At
              least, [He produces a key from his pocket,
              numbly] without a key. [He returns it]

OLIVER   Nice of you to let me in, then. What
              of the ceiling? The floors?

KILLIAN   As thick as the walls. We had the
              whole thing overconstructed. It was never
              meant for a coffin.

VERONICA   What is mine doing in here, then?

KILLIAN   Your death was unexpected. We wanted a quick interment after your – after your passing this morning.

VERONICA   How soon after was I buried?

KILLIAN   We had to wait for nightfall.

VERONICA   Why?

KILLIAN   They regulate funerals for . . . this type of death.

VERONICA   [A pause] Who was in attendance?

KILLIAN   The hearseman, one of his hands, your father, and I.

VERONICA   Is that all? Is that what I've earned with my life?

KILLIAN   Veronica, it was a suicide.

VERONICA   *Suicide.* Curse whoever gave it such a pretty-sounding name.

OLIVER   Someone will hear us, a passerby. That's the way we'll leave.

KILLIAN   We're in the middle of seventy high-walled acres, grave-robber. Someone would have to scale that wall with the specific intention of stealing the daughter of Master Swan. He would have to press his thieving ear against the airtight chink of that iron door there, and we'd have to be screaming our loudest at that very moment.

OLIVER   Then you suspect we'd be discovered?

KILLIAN   Then our ungodly deaths in here would be doubly ironic.

VERONICA   [A pause] How is it I survived the rope?

KILLIAN   What?

VERONICA   How am I alive?

KILLIAN   I . . . suppose I must have found you
            in time.

VERONICA   You were in the house when it
            happened?

KILLIAN   Sitting at your father's desk.

VERONICA   Even on the morning of our
            marriage, Killian?

KILLIAN   There was work yet! A line of people
            at the house to reserve plots at Kingstead, and . . .

VERONICA   And?

KILLIAN   And as I was watching them sign
            their names and accepting their prepayments,
            I felt the floorboards beneath me give a bit.

VERONICA   Give?

KILLIAN   They buckled a bit, yes. Below my
feet I felt this *motion*, as of a sudden weight
applied from underneath. I went to the
basement, and found you hanging from the
rafter just below your father's desk, ready in
your wedding dress. [He absentmindedly
touches his chest pocket. Veronica notices
this]

OLIVER   [A pause. To himself] I need . . . [He
starts at their sudden attention] I need to get to
Halifax.

KILLIAN   For your soul, is it?

OLIVER   My soul, yes.

VERONICA   How did you and it become
separated, resurrectionist?

OLIVER   I was in your same position, miss.

VERONICA   Trapped in a tomb?

OLIVER   Buried alive, in Halifax, [A pause]
                but you don't want to hear the ramblings of a
                man in half. [He scratches the portion of the
                scar on his forehead]

VERONICA   We've ample time for you to tell the
                epic.

OLIVER   I thought I'd found the last of my
                audience a long time ago. [Thinking again] No,
                it's all a bit private, and a tale too bloody for a
                lady's ears.

KILLIAN   Then let's not tell it.

VERONICA   A lady sees more blood in her life
                than any man. I do insist. [Sitting upon her
                coffin]

OLIVER   [A pause] It starts, I suppose, with
                Amy, and so with my starvation.

KILLIAN   Amy, you said? [He and Veronica exchange a look] In Halifax?

OLIVER   In London, I was in London then. [Suddenly attentive, Killian joins Veronica on the coffin] It was twenty years ago, the summer of 1812, me a beggar at fourteen, and for the third day in a row I'd gone without bread. People liked to give their money to the younger children, who weren't inclined to share it with their competition. Now, a day without food, even two, was tolerable. The next day you'd simply beg with twice the haste, and buy your bread then. But three days without, the other street children had warned me of three days without. After three, you'd be too tired to beg again the next day. It was true what they said. The fourth morning, I limped to the peak of the bridge I'd slept beneath, and collapsed in an unmoving heap. [He limps, then collapses on the stage, and proceeds to act out certain parts of the story] That was the trick - moving meant energy, stillness meant surviving. People walked around me, but I was too weak by then to ask for anything. [A pause] At last an angel's raspy voice called down to me. 'Hello? Hello, beggar, are you sleeping?' I rolled up my eyes to see a girl about my age above me, carrying a basket of what I couldn't see. 'Starving,' I said. 'Bread? Money?' 'I've neither, boy,' she told me, 'sorry.' I watched her start to leave but pause, then she took a rock of chalk from a pocket in her tattered dress, and bent to write a message on the stone around me. 'Starving,' she read when finished. She took a sprig of lavender from the basket she had, tucked it around my ear, and left. In minutes more, I slept. Do you know what awoke me?

VERONICA   The girl again?

OLIVER   A golden guinea.

KILLIAN   For a beggar boy? You're lying.

OLIVER   'I'm sorry, Son,' came the gentleman's silvery voice who'd dropped it before me. I rolled up my eyes again to see the back of the man as he left. I tried to rise after him, but a thistle twisted in my stomach and I curled up again. I put the guinea in my mouth to protect it from the other children, too weak just then for any other movement, and I slept. Again, I was awoken.

VERONICA   Another guinea?

OLIVER   The girl again. The sun had all but left behind us as she knelt above me. 'Any pennies, then?' she asked in her rasp. I motioned her near with a flick of my finger, and when she got close enough, I grabbed her shoulder and kissed her. I wish I could've known beforehand what her face would express, spitting the golden guinea out into her own hand. I would've taken better notice when it happened. 'Have this,' she said, shocked, plugging my own mouth with a palmfull of bread. She'd saved it, she said, for me. 'Have your money back, beggar,' and she pressed the guinea into my hand. Before she left, I asked her name.

VERONICA   Amy?

OLIVER   Yes, 'Amy,' she said. [He rises] And when I got my strength, I started roaming London's streets, to pay her back for the bread at least. She was a flower girl, I figured, so I followed every shout of flowers I could. I must have met a dozen different sellers. I'd decided to search until I'd eaten the guinea's worth of bread doing so. Thankfully, plenty money remained when I spied a lavender bouquet, waving back and forth throughout the air, above the heads of passerby. When I went in its direction, I saw a lady stopping to talk to the generous girl I'd met. This lady, she had little beads for eyes, and was asking two bushels for the price of one. Amy seemed ready to concede. 'I'm sorry, ma'am,' I interrupted, 'you'll have to find another seller for a deal such as that. These bushels are worth every penny, ma'am. You'll not find that shade of lavender at any market,' I said. 'And their perfect smell, that's from how they're prepared, ma'am.' Poor Amy looked embarrassed half to death, recognizing me by then. 'And how are they prepared, young man?' the lady asked. 'Tea, ma'am,' I invented. 'We water them with tea when they're young enough to benefit.'

VERONICA   Did the lady buy it?

OLIVER   Two bushels, full price.

VERONICA   Brilliant!

OLIVER   Amy clapped me on the back when the bead-eyed lady had left. The rest of the day we sold together, me perhaps doubling or tripling her profits. At fifteen, she'd already shouted her voice away, and so had only been waving her bouquet. All the other vendors

34

shouted louder than me the same, so I whistled for attention. Another American war was just beginning, see, so I knew the song the people wanted. [He whistles the refrain of "Rule, Britannia!"]

VERONICA   *Rule, Britannia!*

OLIVER   That's the song, yes! They loved it, and never asked what it had to do with lavender. Amy and I might've heard that song a hundred thousand times over the months we spent together.

VERONICA   Months!

OLIVER   Every morning after that first, we'd meet on Amy's corner, Holt and Indiana. We each started wearing a bit of purple ribbon round our sleeves, so the buyers could know us by it. I took up lodgings down the street with a bit of my guinea, and started asking Amy to move in with me. Hers was a lodging house for ladies only, see. It wasn't till the summer's end, on August 26 when I turned fifteen, that she bought me a pastry after selling, said she'd told the ladies, and came home with me. We had a cot and our own corner room for my guinea, though the space *was* a bit . . . dingy. She ended up with lice from the mattress, poor thing, and all so I could maybe save a penny on lodging. I tried to stretch that guinea, see. She cried when I helped her cut the lengths of her hair, thinking people wouldn't buy if they thought her dirty. She kept her head quite covered after that, unless she was in front of only me. That's why I thought you Amy, miss, when I saw you in the coffin. Short hair and the raspiness, you two were quite a bit alike.

VERONICA   I'm sorry, resurrectionist. I am.

OLIVER   Quite, quite alright. [Absently] It's happened before actually, me mistaking another girl for Amy. Shortly after my return from Halifax, actually, but I digress. By early autumn, I realized I'd fallen madly in love with two different women. The first was Amy, the second, a dream of glory on the sea. It was that song I was always whistling! I wanted songs about *me*. I wanted myself to *rule the waves*. I started talking often of the Royal Navy. She never liked to hear it, Amy, but I knew she wasn't happy with the working life a single guinea had provided. One night, I made her three promises: I'd return to London within a year of when I left it for the ocean, I'd come back a captain, and we'd be married then. [A pause] Only one was kept.

VERONICA   Which?

OLIVER   Listen, miss, listen. The next morning, I gave my name to a gentleman from the Marine Society, who said there was a naval ship leaving Portsmouth in less than two weeks' time. I notified the lodging house on Indiana of our moving out, and walked to the corner where Amy and I had stood since summer. I asked her for but a sprig of lavender. It was the first of November, and she was selling her supply dried by that time. She tucked the sprig behind my ear, and I paid her three crowns and a shilling.

KILLIAN   For a single sprig!

OLIVER   For a year's stay at that lodging house with only ladies. It was everything we had, and Amy knew what it meant. Her eyes and mine grew wet. 'Don't let them bury you over there, Oliver Best,' she said, 'you're the best man I've ever met.' 'Two bushels, please,' came a lady's voice behind me. It was the same bead-eyed lady who'd wanted one free, on the first day I'd found Amy selling! 'Twopence,' said Amy, and the lady opened her purse to pay the price in full. In my head, I'm still leaving them both in the crowd behind me, that lady and Amy, whistling *Rule, Britannia!* as I go. [A pause] That night, I lodged with the other Marine Society boys, and in the morning, six of us were taken for free to Portsmouth and our futures in the Navy. [A pause] The *Java* was our ship. We were to convoy a general to Bombay — in India, they said — a governor who'd been appointed. It was the twelfth of November when we left. Wishing to get noticed by the captain — Lambert was the man — I spent whatever hours I could on deck. [He stands stiffly for a moment] 'Captain!' I called at last, impatient, when I saw him on the quarterdeck, 'Captain Lambert!' and I had his attention. 'What? What is it, boy?' the captain called back. He seemed annoyed, a busy man. 'What would you have me be doing, Captain?' I asked. I heard another boy behind me hissing 'Idiot!' but I never understood that. The captain's the one in control, yet the boys were always going to each other with their questions. 'You see that mast, boy?' The captain pointed out the largest of the wooden pillars sprouting up above us. 'Aye, Captain!' I said, for I'd heard another sailor say that to him. 'I want you on the top of it,' Lambert shouted, 'and you'll call down should you see another ship!' 'Aye, Captain!' I shouted back. I went belowdecks to our provisions then, and asked a sailor there for a blanket and two loaves of bread. 'Captain Lambert's orders,' I told him. Two whole loaves, and he gave me them! Oh, but they must have had a hundred casks of it! I took my blanket and my bread, and climbed the rigging of the mast the captain had pointed. [He mimics the ascent] There was a short crosspiece of wood at the top of it, so I swung a leg around either side of it and rode that mast like a stepfather's shoulders and neck. It was windy on the mainmast, but I wrapped my blanket tight and sat. For three days at a time I'd last with my blanket and bread, then I'd crawl back down completely filthy, ravaged by the sun and wind, and ask for two more loaves of it.

VERONICA   Were you not afraid of the height of the mast?

OLIVER   Not much. I *was* quite afraid of

seeing another ship. Or, afraid and excited, perhaps.

VERONICA   And did you? See any other ships?

OLIVER   Many times I thought I did, trained so intent on the horizon. [He scans above the audience] I started seeing them more and more frequent, but would blink and they'd vanish, so I was *blinking* more and more frequent. The sailor who supplied my bread — he was always belowdecks, checking the provisions — he started saying I looked nervous. I'd grip the mast in my sleep [He mimics this action] and dream of endless enemies on the horizon, a wall of them in all directions. Thirteen trips up the mast I had completed, when the enemy was spotted at last. Oh, there was a merchantman before that, spotted once when I'd crawled down for bread, but this was the real villain. We were nearly at December's end, headed for the land of Saint Salvador, they said, for resupply, when I couldn't blink away one of the ships

41

OLIVER   No. I think it was a musket, from
what I saw above the flags and sails. The loud-
mouthed man, he likewise clung to his life
and mast, until the base of it did finally snap
from cannon. I caught his vacant gaze the
moment before he plummeted to the deck. [A
pause] At last, His Majesty's Ship the *Java* was
surrendered, mine by then the only surviving
mast. I climbed down from it to avoid my
neighbor's fate and nearly met an American
bayonet. A score of them had boarded, and
were rounding us up to take us aboard the
Constitution. I saw the loud-mouthed man
on deck, his loud mouth still open. He'd fallen
on his back, and blood had filled his throat
to the lips. 'Now there's a man,' I thought,
'who's dead.' The other boys were whispering
of courts martial for giving up the ship. 'The
lot of us,' one said, 'will be hanged if we make
it back to Britain.' I heard an American accent
mutter something of Commodore Bainbridge
then, and a plan struck my head. I hadn't heard
the name Bainbridge before, but I knew the

word commodore, and so I started screaming them both together. 'Commodore Bainbridge! Commodore Bainbridge!' as if in the crowd, I'd recognized an old friend. And I didn't stop, not when my head was met with the butt of an American musket, not when I was thrown into the bottom of the only boat they had left to transport captives, and not when I was dragged aboard the deck of the *Constitution*. 'Commodore Bainbridge!' I could barely see for the bleeding wound in my head, could barely see him when I was thrown at the feet of the man. [He falls to his knees] He had a gash in each of his legs, both bleeding insanely, but the man still stood, and proudly. 'What is it you want?' he asked me simply, to which I looked up at him, wiped the blood from my lips, and said 'Make me American.'

KILLIAN   What, you deserted?

OLIVER   I thought I might have better luck in the states, yes. [Rising and brushing himself off] He sent me to his purser — Robert Ludlow — to have my name added to the muster of the *Constitution*. When Ludlow asked me who I was, from behind the tiny desk in his cabin, I told him 'My name is Oliver Best. Commodore Bainbridge himself has insisted that I join this ship.' 'Best, is it?' he asked with a grin, then advised me to find another surname, in case my desertion should be discovered by the Brits. 'Oliver Coffin, then,' I said, and he wrote it.

KILLIAN   Coffin? [He and Veronica exchange another look]

OLIVER   The first name that came, yes. And Ludlow said then that he'd like an assistant, 'But never speak, boy,' he advised me, 'outside of this cabin. Yours is a revealing accent, and I won't have you treated different.' To celebrate the new year, he had me follow him to the quarterdeck to watch as the *Java* was set ablaze. The flames must have found her powder, and the ship exploded! 'Congratulations,

American,' Ludlow said, and clapped me on the back. The prisoner Britons were left on parole at Saint Salvador, while we began a nearly two-month limp in the *Constitution* for repairs in Boston. I got to know Ludlow well in his cabin. We spoke of glory, God, and the women who had us. 'Absolutely trapped,' he'd laugh, 'and loving it.' He was a companion to me then, as no man had ever been in all of Britain. When in Boston at last, he introduced me to his brother Augustus. 'Augustus,' he said, 'this is Oliver Coffin, a man with a plan.' Augustus was the Acting First Lieutenant of the *Chesapeake*, another warship in Boston. While *Robert* Ludlow was engaged with the *Constitution*'s reparations, me and *Augustus* would inspect *his* ship, and the men who'd soon sail upon it. He'd introduce me as his youngest brother, 'dumb, but a brilliant seaman.' I later met the *Chesapeake*'s captain, James Lawrence. Augustus would tell me in private of the man's inexperience. Indeed, every evening of that peaceful spring, Robert, Augustus, and myself would gather to eat and speak of the sea. At the end of May, a British ship was seen in the harbor, and Augustus told us that Captain Lawrence intended to meet it. 'Tonight's my last on land,' he said. I insisted that he take me with. 'He makes a fine assistant,' Robert said to Augustus, then 'You protect my brother' to me, with a wink. On the first of June, I stood beside Augustus as our ship approached the *HMS Shannon*. She was a rusty craft, all wood exposed beneath the paint the weather had chipped, and ours, the *Chesapeake,* was a gleaming ship. I knew we'd win, I felt it, standing beside Augustus. [A pause] The battle was over in perhaps ten minutes.

VERONICA   The *Shannon* was taken?

KILLIAN   The *Chesapeake*.

OLIVER   Yes, the *Chesapeake*, miss. I saw the *Shannon*'s discharges pass through the groin and leg of Captain Lawrence, heard him shouting 'Don't give up the ship!' as he was carried broken belowdecks, felt the British grenades and grapeshot dismantle our deck. I saw half the men standing there levelled in an instant, watched the unrelenting Augustus twice wounded by a musket and cutlass, as Broke, the enemy captain, and his men leapt across a narrow band of sea to board our ship. He looked like a titan, that furious captain. I shuddered as I helped assist Ludlow belowdecks. Yes, miss, the *Chesapeake* was taken. Both ships were guided then towards Halifax. For the five-day journey, Augustus and I had been transported to the *Shannon*. He'd insisted I, his brother, follow him. We were situated in a cabin a deck below that of the injured enemy captain, Broke. They said the man's head had been split in half with a sabre on the *Chesapeake*'s deck. The night before we landed in Halifax, as Augustus slept, I crept up to the dying captain's cabin, wanting again to see the titan. He wore a hundred bandages about his head, and shifted restless in his bed. I took his hand and he paused, his eyes screwed shut in pain or confusion. 'Captain Broke,' I whispered to him, with my first words spoken to a non-Ludlow in almost half a year, 'while *Shannon* moves, you live.' Through his sort of sleep, he squeezed my hand lightly, and I left him. Augustus was hospitalized in Halifax, me at his silent bedside all the while. Within a few days, I awoke from my seat beside him to find him dead. Thought to be his American brother, I was transported then to join the rest of the *Chesapeake* prisoners.

VERONICA   Where were you taken?

OLIVER   Melville Island. [A pause] There was a massive room they'd built for all their prisoner men, maybe a thousand of us, from a hundred different ships. We slept in hammocks slung four high, swinging between the pillars of the cattle barn construction. The men would sob and moan and curse the British. Of course, I never said a word to any of them, for my accent. I spent what time I could inside my hammock, [He sits and leans against the marble base] fourth from the ground, thinking numbly of the Ludlow brothers. The first of every month, at daybreak, the man who slept beneath me would poke the bottom of my hammock. I'd swing my head over to look at him, and he'd say the same thing - the name of the month and 'It helps you going, knowing.' Then he'd lean over and tell the man beneath *him*. I heard this calendar man speak 'July,' 'August,' 'September,' 'October - It helps you going, knowing.' That's the first time in Halifax I thought of Amy, October first, and my promises to her. [Standing] When we were all brought out by the guards that morning to stand in the wind, needlessly shivering, I took a look about me. A simple picket fence surrounded the yard, one short enough, I thought, for me to climb in seconds. Of course, by the time I ran there from the barn, a hundred bullets from the island garrison would have my back. [A pause] Still looking around, I noticed a few wooden buildings of the Melville Island plateau besides our heavily-guarded own, one of which contained a hospital for injured captives. And that hospital they had, the way I saw it, was outside the fence and a few steps from freedom. I decided then to get myself beaten to the point of hospitalization, then make a run for it. I nudged the calendar man, who stood beside me likewise shivering, and pointed out who looked to be the meanest creature on the island, a man who stood a hundred yards away, separated some from the rest of the prisoner company. 'Thomas Swaine,' the calendar began, 'is here because he put a bullet through a poor farmer's head, ransacked his home, and abused his family's womenfolk. He couldn't give a single reason for it.' [A pause] 'Perfect,' I thought, and without hesitation walked up behind this Swaine, smacked him over the top of his head, and said 'Dance.' [If performed by a non-English company, this word alone is spoken in an English accent] 'Dance,' the first word I'd spoken on Melville Island, and it gave away my accent. 'Whose side,' Swaine said, with a hand around my neck, 'do you represent?' 'I get up every morning and pick a different, pig Swain,' I chokingly responded. He took a penny knife from his waist and said 'This blade is blessed. When we're done, I'll have your tongue, and the Devil will know none of it. You're split.' And with that, quicker than any whip, he stabbed the blade into the nape of my neck, brought it up around my wriggling head, and down the front to my chest. [He falls, squirming, to his back] He would've kept, had my screams and bleeding not earned the guardsmen's notice. He dropped the knife when they tackled him. That's this, [He takes a blade from his boot] and this. [If wearing a hat, the actor removes it. He traces with the blade the scar on his head and face] I slid the knife in my waist the same, and was dragged to the surgeons from there. Oh, they stitched me up right, it took half the day, but as I thrashed about on the table they'd laid, I noticed an awful lot of soldiers looking in from outside. Escape wasn't likely this way, I decided, but I didn't want my efforts gone to waste. I thought of the loud-mouthed man on the *Java*'s foremast, [A pause] then I thought of him on the deck. When I found a moment with the surgeons outside for breath, me left to recover, I took the penny knife and split a few of the stitches keeping together my upper lip, then stretched it apart and started bleeding intense all over again. With my neck cocked, I collected all of it into my mouth so it pooled at the back. When the surgeon's boy-assistant walked in and past, I started gurgling it. Well, he ran out for the surgeon, and I set my eyes with the same vacant gaze I'd seen on the loud-mouthed man. I was bagged in sackcloth then, and shortly hoisted into what I felt to be an open carriage. I couldn't discern the words of the horsemen, for the noise of that carriage as we went, but from the different sentence sounds decided there were two of them. We rode for ten minutes perhaps, when they stopped the horses and stepped from the carriage. I heard the sound of shovels then. I thought of cutting myself out from the sack and running from them while they were engaged, but pictured two muskets and two bayonets. Instead, I brought my forearms a few inches from my face, [He does so, holding the blade] squirming to give myself some space in the sack. Then *stillness meant surviving.* They dragged me from the cart by the bagged head, and rolled me into the hole they'd dug. I landed on my left. They made quick work of replacing the earth then, thankfully starting with my feet, to give me one last breath through the sack before burying my head. It felt like a heavy leaden blanket. They whacked the dirt above me with their shovel backs, and I felt the earth rumble as they left. [A pause] That was my burial, October first, 1813. [A pause] My breaths were shallow, humid. All smelled of worms and putrification. When I no longer felt the carriage, I brought the blade down to my hips to cut the sack they'd given. [He does so, the sack imagined] Then it was a kicking and stretching, and when my hands felt the cool air, I knew I was free. Couldn't have been more than a few feet deep. [Sitting up] When I unearthed my head, I saw the carriage far off and leaving. They hadn't marked the grave, I noticed, and there were a few other patches of loose dirt about me, like they made burying prisoners a practice in that place. Melville's barn was off to my right. I watched it glow in what was left of the sunset. I was all blood and mud then, and cut in half, so waited for the light to end before beginning my trek. I needed a ship for Britain, but didn't know the scape of Halifax. [He stands] And so, having crawled from my grave and its own plateau, I stumbled in the shadows until I found another person. A man enjoyed a pipe from his house's front steps, and I asked him from a lightless patch for the dockyard's direction. He gave it, yet seven more times that night I had to ask instruction from the startled men of Halifax, and in three hours' time, perhaps, I found myself before the home of the Honorable

Wodehouse, commissioner, they said, of the dockyard. The windows of a lower room were lighted. A man inside had his back to me, and a scarf about his head. 'Wodehouse!' I called up to him, but when he craned his neck to inspect, I saw it wasn't him.

KILLIAN   How could you have known Wodehouse's appearance?

OLIVER   I didn't know Wodehouse, I knew the man.

VERONICA   Who was it?

OLIVER   Broke, Captain Broke of the *Shannon*. He'd survived the sabre injury he'd taken to the head. Wodehouse himself appeared at the front door then, screaming for quiet and to give the captain his rest. When he approached me with a lamp, he saw my condition and nearly fell back. 'Captain! Captain!' I shouted at the window above us.

'While *Shannon* moves, you live!' Well, that captured the captain's attention. He opened the window and demanded Wodehouse let me in. The captain asked who I was once shivering indoors, but I told him only that I'd sailed with him upon the *Shannon*. He said I'd given him strength, and I asked him for it back. 'Is that why you've come, Son? For strength?' Wodehouse interrupted. 'I came for glory,' I told them both, 'but now would rather be back in London.' As it so happened, Broke was leaving in three days' time for Britain, and really did request that I join him. He had me cleaned, new-clothed, my lip re-stitched. On October fourth, I escorted Broke back onto the deck of his ship. 'While *Shannon* moves, I am alive!' he shouted to his men. The look of us, his pirate's bandana, my scars of a pirate, struck fear into the hearts of the lot of them. We spent the voyage in his cabin, and told each other of the women we'd left waiting, he of his wife Louisa and their children, me of Amy. When I asked for advice on being a husband, he told me 'When alone, a man and his wife should be completely naked with each other.' That's how he described it, nakedness. Often, he would have to pause our talk and rest. I hadn't imagined a titan could be such a gentle man. We landed at Portsmouth on November second to a scene of celebration. He offered a seat beside him that day in a coach back to London, and what you've heard here is the tale I told him on the way. I've only ever told it twice - then and today. 'Steadfast, Son, steadfast,' he called me proudly as our carriage halted outside of London's Admiralty, 'but a deserter all the same. What again was your surname? I'll tell your tale after I've seen you hang.' 'Coffin,' I said, 'Oliver Coffin, Captain, but you'll never see me again.' With that, I slipped from the carriage and down the street. He made no effort to stop me.

VERONICA   And did you find Amy?

OLIVER   I looked for her at Holt and Indiana

the following morning, where another, younger dry lavender seller told me sadly that I'd find her sleeping at Saint Augustine, 'in the churchyard,' she told me, and with the sickest feeling in my stomach I ran in the direction she was pointing. The steeple rose above me soon, and at the gate of the graves I hunched a moment, panting. [He does so] That's when I saw her, her hair again aplenty, wearing all blacks and greys and standing above a grave with what looked to be a babe. 'Amy! Amy!' I screamed, and she looked over at me, quite surprised and silently. As I approached, still claiming her name, I watched a look of horror twist her face, then weeping well up, then a lot of head shaking. 'Amy.' [He falls to his knees] I whispered it practically, falling at her feet. She only pointed to the stone behind me, at the freshest and shortest etching on it specifically. 'What, what does it say?' I asked her, staring in confusion at the sharpness of the word. [A pause] 'Amy,' came a man's silvery voice above me. 'That's the Coffin stone. Amy was added three months ago,' the man's voice told me. I looked up to see a sexton, standing with his hand upon the shoulder I had thought was Amy's. She'd never mentioned a sister, much less a twin.

VERONICA   Are you quite serious, resurrectionist? Killian? [Killian rises and starts pacing slowly behind the coffin]

OLIVER   Yes, miss, I was looking up at your parents.

VERONICA   Killian?

OLIVER   Every day, [He falls to his side] every single day I spent above her grave, laying above it, listening, and every night I did the same. Through rain, or wind, or snow, I lied upon it. The sexton Swan would bring me daily bread and blankets. When I asked when his wife would visit again, he said she'd taken sick. 'I wish I'd do the same,' I said, 'to pass and see Amy again,' but I wouldn't. [A pause. He stands] After six months, six months of lying there, in the spring, he came to me and said his wife was dead. Because there wasn't a Swan stone in the churchyard — the sexton had said he'd come alone from another land — she would be buried above her sister under the stone marked *Coffin*. There another name he scratched. 'Jan,' he read. [Killian pauses a moment, then continues pacing] He told me something else then. 'When Amy was ill this way,' he said, 'she wrote a letter to one Oliver Best, a navy man.' Because the *Java*'s crew had been returned, Jan had read, and yet I hadn't come, she'd imagined me dead. However, she kept this information from her twin, not to worsen Amy's condition in their ladies-only lodging bed, and so promised to mail the letter. Instead, Jan buried her sister with it. She met the sexton Swan on the day of the interment. He told me this, and said because the grave would be reopened in adding Jan's coffin, I'd have an opportunity to retrieve what Amy had written. 'And when you see her at peace that way,' he told me, 'you can always think of her as only sleeping, never dead.' [A pause. He returns to his knees] When I pried open my lover's cheap and rotting coffin lid, I found her perfectly preserved inside of it. Her face was ashen, yet looked as if for nine months she had only slept. I leaned in, entranced, to brush a finger cross her marble forehead, [A pause] but my knuckle slipped clean through the flesh and against the skull beneath it. It was grave wax that had covered my beloved. I became quite aware then of the foul, rotting stench. Horrified, I took from the folded hands above her sunken chest a tattered slip of parchment, [He takes a letter from his chest pocket] this. [Killian again pauses a moment, and touches his chest. Veronica notices] And suddenly, friends, I saw the grave as desecrated, and did begin to panic. Not wanting her to tell the Devil on me, I grabbed the blessed penny blade from my boot, opened her rotting mouth, and cut the tongue from it. [A pause. He rises again] I did the same to her sister when we buried Jan's empty coffin, dragging her body instead for sale to the anatomists. See, the sexton had decided he could make a double profit from the bodies brought to him, once from the family, once from the students. I wasn't much inclined to it for the moral ramifications, but he pointed out I'd already raided the grave of my beloved. We've emptied every Saint Augustine coffin ever since, me cutting the tongues from every one of them.

VERONICA   Good God. My mother, stolen? Good God. Is my father this monster of a man?

OLIVER   The Owl always loved you, miss. Very protective. Why, the day I met him, above Amy, your weeping mother offered me her babe, but your father, he immediately snatched you from her, scowling. Very protective, I say. [To himself] Inspiring.

VERONICA   My mother never held me.

OLIVER What do you mean?

VERONICA She died as I was born, the bloodline's destiny.

OLIVER Excuse me?

VERONICA Every woman from my mother's family dies with the birth of her first babe. For generations, it's happened. Jan and Amy were the first siblings of the thin family tree, because they were born at once of the same dead woman.

OLIVER But you're mistaken. I saw your mother offer you above her sister's grave.

VERONICA [A pause] Resurrectionist, that letter, what does it say?

OLIVER The day I got it, the Owl read it to me. [Smiling] He said, 'She loved you very much, but she's taken sick, and get back safely.' I've kept it since for Amy to protect me, scanning over her stout, pretty lettering when I'm alone and missing.

VERONICA   Would you mind, resurrectionist, would you mind if I read it?

OLIVER   Oh, I don't mind. It's proper, with you looking so like the author. [He hands her the letter and takes Killian's place on the coffin. Killian himself ceases pacing once the letter has begun]

VERONICA   'Oliver, my hero sailor, captain of whatever ship you've picked to capture, I've got another reason for your safe return. A child, Oliver! I'm pregnant! God bless us, I'm pregnant! And he wants to meet his father-captain. Come home, and love him, and we'll be wed this time. Oliver, Oliver, I feel alive.'

OLIVER   A child? [A pause] Pregnant.

VERONICA   You two have met. [She looks at Killian] When he took the babe in, my father named him Killian, but left him his mother's surname, for me to take at marriage.

OLIVER   Coffin?

KILLIAN   Coffin.

OLIVER   My son . . . I wish I would've known. I wish . . . I wish I would've known. I spent a lot of time living like a man without a son.

KILLIAN   You are one. I was never told much of my parents. [A pause] I have none. And after your tale, I'm glad.

VERONICA   Killian!

KILLIAN   I'm no beggar. I sell no lavender. No! I am a Kingstead Cemetery partner! When Master Swan retires, I will be the sole owner! You, *sir*, are nothing more than the muscle he hired, probably insane, your story fabricated.

VERONICA	Killian, please!

KILLIAN	He cuts the tongues from the dead!
You think him a rational man?

OLIVER	[Distracted] So the Devil wouldn't
know what the dead have seen.

KILLIAN	The Devil knows everything.

OLIVER	No, no, that's God you're thinking.
The Devil hears it from his sinners.

KILLIAN	Hellions can't say a single thing.

OLIVER	Why's that you speak?

KILLIAN	Their mouths are full of the fat
black pearls they eat at the feast of the Devil,
the pearls of trouble and deceit.

OLIVER   They'd spit them out, I swear they'd spit them out for me. They'd tell and bite and torture me.

KILLIAN   Maybe, grave thief, what you deserve is coming.

OLIVER   [A pause] Can I tell you something? [Pointing to Veronica briefly, rising from his seat] Outside of her tomb I may be a thief, and you a partner, and she a lady. But inside the Swan Tomb we are all three nothing. And you will die, and she will die, and I . . . and I will be in here alive forever.

VERONICA   Resurrectionist, what do you mean?

OLIVER   I've no soul, miss. My soul, I said, was left in Halifax. On the first of October, 1813, I was separated from it. The Earth, she had me then, and failed to give all of me back. Now no sickness, no death.

KILLIAN   Rational, I ask?

VERONICA   How did you intend to retrieve it?

OLIVER   I erred in letting them bury me, I've
     decided. Once the Earth envelops you, you're
     supposed to stay dead. After I'd taken you from
     your coffin, I intended to sail back to Halifax,
     find the island I'd been buried in, dig up my
     unmarked grave again, and crawl inside of it.

VERONICA   To die?

OLIVER   To die. [A pause] I was made in
     violence, born in violence, lived in violence,
     and now, miss, and now I want to rest. Until I
     and my soul are reunited, it will never happen,
     and I'll never see Amy again. You two will
     die, and I'll be trapped in here with whatever
     crawls up from the Devil's sands.

KILLIAN   Absolutely mad. This man is
     absolutely mad.

VERONICA   Why did you stay for my body, resurrectionist?

OLIVER   I didn't at first intend it. In fact, had I not decided, I would this instant be headed for Portsmouth again. But when a rumor spread this morning of the death of the daughter of Kingstead, I started thinking what the Owl owed me. For twenty years nearly, I dug up his graves and carried his bodies, and all for only a couple crowns of what we were paid. He was always saying he needed it, for the family.

KILLIAN   Why work for him, then?

OLIVER   Digging beats begging. 'But for once,' I thought, once the rumor slithered in, 'I'll get the lot, and I'll get it for his daughter. He'll pay me in his own flesh and blood.'

VERONICA   My mother, he sold my mother, didn't you say. I hardly think he'd mind about my missing.

OLIVER   Regardless of the injured's opinion,
    an injury's an injury.

VERONICA   [A pause] What am I worth?

OLIVER   Come again?

VERONICA   How much would you have gotten
    for me?

OLIVER   Pretty young thing? Nine or ten
    guineas.

VERONICA   And you'd only see a couple crowns
    of that fee?

OLIVER   That half-a-mansion you're living
    in wasn't rented on a sexton's salary.

VERONICA   [Rising from her seat] You must
    have known of the robberies then, Killian,
    [Bitterly] you so involved with Father's
    business since our adolescence.

KILLIAN   [A pause] He never told me his hand was a madman.

OLIVER   You were raised together by him, is that it?

VERONICA   As cousins, yes. [A pause] He told us very early that he intended for us to wed, and for Killian to learn his work as a sexton. But Killian and I, we made ourselves a promise. [To Killian] Remember it? The day we married, we would leave behind forever London, and the yard of Saint Augustine.

OLIVER   [A pause] Then why are we here today? What happened?

VERONICA   It was . . . It was *Kingstead*. Father started talking of the cemetery business, and Killian bought into his plan of riches.

KILLIAN   I didn't!

VERONICA   He'd tell me 'Veronica, perhaps just a few more years in London after the marriage, just a bit more money in our pockets.' But I didn't care if we had any, Killian. I told you that. I didn't need to be rich, I just wanted out of London.

KILLIAN   To raise a family on a pittance!

VERONICA   That's it! That's just how *he* started talking! You knew I never wanted children, but would go on anyway about an *heir* to this Kingstead business.

KILLIAN   You kept me from them, my children.

VERONICA   An infant would have killed me, Killian! You know!

KILLIAN   There is no knowing!

VERONICA   [A pause] Soon it was clear that I

was trapped in London. That must have been my reason, wasn't it, Killian? For tying that rope around my neck? I'm sure that I was *glad* to do it.

KILLIAN   You lie!

VERONICA   I'm sure that I was glad to die!

KILLIAN   You didn't see your eyes!

VERONICA   [A pause] When?

KILLIAN   What were you thinking, swinging there? What were you thinking!

VERONICA   My eyes?

KILLIAN   [Walking toward her] You were alive yet when I sat in the basement, and I watched you kick, and I waited. And with your eyes, Veronica, with your eyes you said 'Save me again. I am an idiot.' [With the knife, she stabs him in the chest. He holds the blade in place as he drops where he stands behind the coffin. Shaken, she stumbles and sits upon the ground before the marble base. Oliver walks behind and looks down at Killian]

OLIVER   What does this mean? For me, I mean. I . . . I've lost a son, is that it? [A pause] Is that it?

VERONICA   If he had no father, you had no son, resurrectionist. And my cousin . . . [She buries her face in her hands. Oliver stoops over Killian a moment, rising with the knife and a severed tongue. He joins Veronica in sitting before the marble base]

OLIVER   You're alright, miss. [They sit in silence, until a confused expression crosses Veronica's countenance, and she rises to likewise stoop behind the coffin. She returns to her seat with a letter in her hand]

VERONICA   His chest pocket. [She unfolds and reads the note] 'Killian, my anchor husband of this afternoon, I am marooned, the image of *you* embossed upon my womb. Pregnant, Killian, pregnant! We fools, we children. I missed the last few months of blood and knew it. What was I to do? Wait for the birth of the brute to die? Let an infant take my life? No, no. I'll die on my own time. The rope is tied behind me. My life — my life! — gone, Killian, delivered, donated, the wife of Death. Cut me down and frame me, Killian. Have my dress. Have the hair you coveted. I myself never wanted this city, this London, this all-consuming infant. Could things not have been different? We could have lived amid the wilderness, the gardens of the forest, if it weren't for your graves and your babe, your scary infant, couldn't we have, Killian? Killian, I wish to die.' [She grabs her stomach] Pregnant?

OLIVER   What – what can we do about it?

VERONICA   What?

OLIVER   Well, it's an innocent, isn't it?

VERONICA   [A pause] Resurrectionist, what's
    going to happen?

OLIVER   Miss, we're trapped.

VERONICA   How will I die, then?

OLIVER   It . . . it'll be a lack of food and
    drink, or air perhaps that brings it.

VERONICA   [A pause] I don't want that.

OLIVER   What?

VERONICA   I don't want to die like that. A . . .
    victim of circumstance.

OLIVER   How . . . how would you like it.

VERONICA   Myself. I'll use my own hand to finish off this incident . . . and Killian's infant.

OLIVER   You're quite sure of that?

VERONICA   [A pause] Are there . . . are there *moral ramifications*? Does God forgive his broken children?

OLIVER   Well sure, sure he does, miss.

VERONICA   How . . . how can I do it? [They peer about] There's a bit of the doorjamb, do we have any rope to tie around it?

OLIVER   We could find something, yes.

VERONICA   Will that be painless?

OLIVER   I don't think so, miss.

VERONICA   What else, then?

OLIVER   There's a minute of that candle left.
          We could - we could light your dress afire.

VERONICA   I think I'm going to be sick.

OLIVER   Or the, the blade, then.

VERONICA   [A pause] Where do I put it?

OLIVER   The heart looked quick.

VERONICA   Oh, God.

OLIVER   The neck.

VERONICA   Oh,   God!   That's   too   close,
          resurrectionist.

OLIVER   [A pause] How about your wrist.

VERONICA   Is that quick?

OLIVER   If you sever quite deep it should be, yes.

VERONICA   [Taking up the blade in her hands, looking at it] I don't think I can do it.

OLIVER   I can help you if you'd like, miss. I can help with it.

VERONICA   I . . .

OLIVER   I can help with it.

VERONICA   [A pause] Should I stand? Or sit?

OLIVER   I think stand, and we'll hang the wound below your heart. [Standing] You want this?

VERONICA   [Standing] I . . . yes.

OLIVER   Let me have your hands. [He stands behind her. With one hand, he grabs her own, which holds the knife. With the other, her opposite wrist] We want to start at the bottom there, and drag upwards like this. [He traces the blade up her forearm] Through the sleeve, so you won't have to see it.

VERONICA   Did it hurt, the scar you got on Melville Island?

OLIVER   The most painful experience.

VERONICA   [A pause] Drag the blade up like that? [She traces her forearm again]

OLIVER   And deep, yes. We'll – we'll put the blade in at the base of your wrist, [A pause] like this. [He punctures her wrist, which starts bleeding around the blade]

VERONICA   [An expression of panic] Re-resurrectionist?

OLIVER   It's just to drag the blade up now,
           miss.

VERONICA   [Panting] Please don't move the
           blade, sir.

OLIVER   You'll – you'll die from even this.
           We'll just finish, so it can be quick.

VERONICA   Please don't move the blade, sir.

OLIVER   Then I'm going to pull your wrist.

VERONICA   [A pause] Oliver?

OLIVER   [A pause] Miss? [A pause. He
           pulls her forearm forward through the blade,
           then drops the implement on the ground. He
           moves her forearm down so the blood can
           flow freely, then begins whistling the refrain
           of "Rule, Britannia!" slowly. They sink to the
           ground. Veronica's head is in his arms, her
           body twitching slightly, though less and less.

By the time Oliver has finished whistling the song's refrain, Veronica lies dead. A pause. Oliver looks at the coffin. He lifts her up and slides her feet-first through the square hole in the lead. He pauses, looking into it, then he retrieves his blade, and his hands disappear inside the hole again. A tongue is brought out from within. He then refolds the lead hatch door and replaces the outer coffin's lid. He picks up what's left of the dying candle and the letter from Amy, sitting centered in front of the marble base, trying to read. Slowly, Killian rises from behind the coffin, on the end opposite Veronica's head, and the audience-facing coffin door opens. Both Killian and Veronica wear black makeup smeared over their closed eyes. Oliver cocks his head slightly to one side, in Killian's direction] Hello? [Killian's eyes snap open, looking directly at Oliver. Killian's mouth slowly opens into a massive grin, and blood and black pearls drool out slowly over his chin and onto the ground. Oliver cocks his head slightly to the other side, in Veronica's direction] Hello? [Veronica's eyes snap open, looking directly at Oliver. Her mouth slowly opens into a massive frown, and blood and golden guineas drool out slowly over the side of her mouth and into the coffin. Still staring at Oliver, Killian moves to grip the coffin's lid, and the lights go black]

www.ingramcontent.com/pod-product-compliance
Lightning Source LLC
Chambersburg PA
CBHW071906020426
42331CB00010B/2702

* 9 7 8 1 6 4 5 3 8 0 1 9 1 *